The Terrestrial Madonna
Our Lady of Desire

A Collection By
Leona Bloom

AuthorHouse™
1663 Liberty Drive
Bloomington, IN 47403
www.authorhouse.com
Phone: 833-262-8899

This book is printed on acid-free paper.

ISBN: 979-8-8230-1549-3 (sc)
979-8-8230-1550-9 (e)

Print information available on the last page.

Published by AuthorHouse 09/27/2023

authorHOUSE®

To God,

WHOM I LOVE DESPITE ME.

I come to you humbly, as a girl torn in spirit and mind synchronously.
I know God, I feel him in the bones of my body and the bones of my ancestors.
I know him in the trees and I see him in the sky. I feel God beckon to me,
he forgives me, and that is all that matters. My forgiveness with him is where
your business comes to an end. The rest is up to me. Although I know God,
I also know my shadow. I know my human desires and I know my need for
material things. I am torn, you see, between this world and the next. I love my
humanity, and I love love. Therefore, I ask, does God condemn sin or condemn
those who ignore it? Those who do not grow spiritually through first mapping
their physical body. Perhaps embracing the body guarantees the flaming forks
of hell. I'd rather die on my own cross, for my God, and know that I lived.

PART ONE

Romans 8:35

The Infernal Realms

Who shall separate us from the love of Christ?
Shall trouble or hardship or persecution or famine or nakedness or danger or sword?

The Sky And The Steeple

When my hand crept along the white steeple, grasping, searching for God, I found that I'd followed a map which led only to a cold sky and adolescent apostasy. As a young girl I'd have raging fits, my round cheeks red and demeanor vengeful, screaming words with vile meaning a child cannot comprehend. I was called a heathen. My sweet grandmother, unbeknownst to her, divined in this word the silence I'd become so familiar with at the end of a prayer. In bed at night I'd find myself on my knees, hands held together tight, in a feverish communion. I could not convince my childish mind to worship a cross, yet I found God among the grit. The instinct to feed, to clean my broken body, that was the miracle to which I felt in awe when beholden. The instinct to rebel when made to lower my eyes to the good book, the gift of the will, the gift of freedom. God is not among the stars, because God is the stars from whence we are made. Why look up at all when the earth holds the hand that feeds us?

Deliverance

If I nail you to a cross
Hanging from hands and feet
Will you let me worship you
From down on both knees
Gasping for more air
While red wine fills my lungs
Drinking the plentiful blood
Of my amorous christ.

Breathe softly into my lips
Let me inhale your holy ghost
Seal my jagged wounds
Inflicted by hellish tormentors
Lay me to deep rest
And perform miraculous resurrection
For I will raise of the pit
To please my amorous christ.

Corpo Di Cristo

Every dreary day, as if by mechanical clockwork
I am beholden to heaven, yet damned never to walk it.
Cosmic gates unfurl as if the petal of a rose
Whose bud may seem near, yet I cannot enclose.
Two glorious stars shine down near my face,
The white light only reaching a red two headed snake.
The roads of New Jerusalem with their voluptuous curves,
My feet have been damned, a trip I'm forbidden to make.
The ripe, pink fruit which my hands yearn to pluck,
My lips are damned for me to never close and suck.
Heaven is desire, tis' my god sanctioned devil.
So I make my bed merrily, and in the silken sheets I lie,
And from my sad purgatory, paradise I shall spy.

Lazurite

A golden haired Lazurite, wreathed wholly in flame
For whom the perpetual grave is an unshakeable friend.
She whose birthright is resurrection and death
And She whose sole purpose is unto herself mend.

Eyes winding in circles as does a cycle
Following close while the snake doth consume,
All creation which rises must one fateful day fall
Prophesied in the snuffing of the Moon.

The greatest deception must be the unending
Yet tis, also an instinctual comfort,
Still the golden haired Lazurite seizes the Void,
As the Void wants for her soul as none other.

Live By The Sword

Torn from His grace, stranded on this plane
Is the battle maiden born of sinner's viscera
Juno's River Styx running crimson and metallic
Feeding to a brutal sea void of heavenly virtue.

She lives by her blade and thorough scale
Lit passionately with forked flaming tongue
For what is a lesson unto us forged
Earned earnestly despite eager whips.

She searches long and far for his restoration
As was foretold inside the votive lamb
Yet no claws can thieve hallowed providence
Leaving in Her wake bruised tears and sighs.

Hell hath not erupt a fury like a woman scorned
Cleaving out from earth a trail of wicked flames
To wreak the rapture one mustn't raise their eyes
But aim true to the sky a savage battle cry.

Sin (Or An Expectation)

I must confess to you, Lord, I am a sinner. For I have gazed upon your creation which took six days and a Sunday of rest, and I have found that I expected more. More of creation, and more of this world.

I sit upon the cool rock which lay on the side of the hill and lift my eyes to the dawning horizon. I await to behold Apollo riding forth on his golden chariot led by silver mares, but am instead met with an austere yellow eye. As my gaze lingers among the clouds, I find the colors not living up to my hopes of a vibrant scape, shaped as white cities among the sky. I feel the air billowing upon my face and am disappointed not to meet Zephyr's blue lips in a passionate embrace. My hands dig deep in the ground, and instead of meeting Gaia, interlocking her fingers with mine, I grasp nothing but dirt, and grime, and pebbles.

As a girl I read wonderful stories of romance and frivolity. A kiss under a gazebo as a storm rolls in over sylvan summits where cottages lie under shaded forest awnings, perfect for a rainy day getaway with a special lover. A legendary hero coming to my rescue as I stand chained to a rock, preparing myself for imminent death, while a great sea beast waits to consume me as a sacrifice for my country. Someone for whom my greatest burden is a cross they voluntarily bear. Lord, why construct such amorous words and forget to create the lips which speak them?

I must confess to you, Lord, I am a sinner. For I once hung tightly to your promise of love, only to discover the truest lover is the only belonging we are born with in this world, and it is found peering back from the mirror. Forgive me.

PART TWO

John 1:9

THE PURGATORIAL REALMS

If we confess our sins, he is faithful and just to forgive us our sins
and to cleanse us from all unrighteousness.

Cruel Mistress

Any tear left unwept is one truly wasted,
Like an unkindness taken flight in the dark
To harass the stars and their gentle observers.
I shall mourn, I shall release a murder
Which centers on one unforgiven in thought.
Unforgiven by the bitter mistress
Who rules my domain and insecurity.
She is the leaves blowing in a breeze, cold and dead.
For if a thought cannot manifest,
Then let an action speak louder,
Lord knows I cannot be the one to speak louder.

What must I do for you to speak?
It's as if each word requires anchor upheaval.
Words not even you can formulate.
Words stuck in a head brimming with madness,
Words which I cannot bear to translate.
In the past they have only left bruises and cuts
And called on she of the dark and lustful.
She pulls on my bars and begs for freedom
Bargaining with tongue which only knows pain,
For even the innocent have stood in her way.
She seeps out a venom which takes no prisoners
And slowly takes over, my cruel mistress.

Crown of Thorns

As best I try, I cannot breathe
Past the vines which hold me,
Trapping all sweet air tight
Unable to enter my lungs.
The leaves weigh on me heavy
A burden I can no longer bear
I beg for a release, yet see none.

Relax young girl, tomorrow is to come.
But how can I with this fear
That they breathe a different air
And know a foreign moon.
For I will only be forgotten
Left to cling to fleeting life
And swallowed in the thorns.

I plead, do not forget me
When a new wind comes to blow
My nails can only take so much
Clawing bloody at the walls.
Only when a new dawn rises
With us mountain lengths apart
Will I retire in my mourning.

Veil of Bereavement

Even when you leave
And I curse your stupid name,
Even when I'm crying
Because you made me
Feel so ashamed,
I hate that I still
Cling to your smell.
I may hate your face,
But love your scent
Like a distant,
Happy memory.
I cherish it dearly.
You wear your old selves
Aroma like a mask
And I am reminded daily
Of they who once were.

An End

I reached to my nightstand this morning
In need of a drink of water
Yet I found my cup barren
With not a drop left behind
And then I remembered in that moment
I'd given all my water to you
With your beautiful, greedy lips
Gulping every last sip
Leaving me parched and dry
Tossed forgotten to the side.

A Beginning

I awoke this morning
To the bright sun
Warming my blue face
It shined me through
And made me tire
Of perpetual melancholy
So I fill my cup
After you drank
All I had to give
And now save it for myself
So one beautiful day
My vessel will burst
And my face will bloom to life.

Pearlescent Alabaster

There was a time
Not long ago
When I took comfort
Only in the moon.
My skin was pale,
My heart was frail
Like alabaster
Reflecting her planetary
Sensitivities.
Yet one day,
The sun came down
Like a statuesque angel.
He took my hand,
And took my heart,
To unthaw as a glacier.
I feel it still, the fire within
Warming up my belly.
Now I rejoice
In the liberation
Of loving all times of day.

PART THREE

John 4:7-8

THE TERRESTRIAL REALMS

Beloved, let us love one another, for love is from God,
and whoever loves has been born of God and knows God.
Anyone who does not love does know God, because God is love.

Cold, Collected Clarity

Her gaze a frost which kills the brush
Of complication and human instability.
For those that bloom in this wild garden
Grow weary of their austere observer.

The garden is of thorns and maws
Which gnash at her gentle caress,
For the petals commune in colors
Which she does not understand.

The blossom at the center glows
Unfurling petals of azure shade
Which strangles with its bristled roots
The garden the observer laid.

She knows the rules of this flower
Which corrupts and plagues her land,
All it knows is how to strangle
Yet she plants it with her two hands.

For when the monster grows and smothers
Despite her hopeless sincerity,
She walks among the ruined garden
Discovering in her soul a cold, collected clarity.

Sacred Alchemy

For how long can
A caterpillar
Fight against
Her own skin
Before bursting
Into colors
Expansive as the dawn
To fly away
On better skies
Riding better winds
Done with crying
Over uneven wings
As she has undergone
A painful metamorphosis

A Kindred Flame

I could not care less
The size of your chest.
I am not bothered,
By what lies between
Your freckled legs.
Man or woman,
Old or young,
I'd fall to my knees
Clasping tightly my hands
At your every mercy
Praying to love.
And pleading, with
Every
Last
Breath
You do the same.

Yours Truly,

"Tell me lover, how did I do?"
They said eyes wide
Bursting with anticipation;
Looking up to me
Grasping their rosary
As if I, a queen high
On my earthly throne.
I look down to their chin
Which glimmers with wetness
"Perfectly, my beloved."
I find my greatest pleasure
In their eyes which shine
With lashes like wisps
Which seek nothing
In this life, nor the next
But my unconditional grace.

Floraphilia

I beckon you, beloved, to my garden
Which I cultivate by hand;
Merry daisies slick the edges
Bordered by an iron fence.

And within the heart lies a rose
Shining with pinkish luster.
Pick the rose, my sacred rose
Slept between twin hedge arches.

Be careful to cut the stem softly,
Or rather rough if you'd prefer,
Ravage it with a ferocity
No man could hope defer.

Treasure this, my fragile rose
Compare it's twinkle to the stars
But I warn thee beloved, do not abuse it
Lest my gentility depart.

Plantae Ecstacia

And from her bountiful palate
Lept great earthly desire
Of an orgasmic longing
To absolutely, wholly devour.

Birthed of terrestrial feminine
Is our saccharine fruits,
And the fragrant delights
Which cause pleasure ensue.

For what is love if not a tree?
Grown in carnal company.
And what is desire if not a flower?
A blessing to one with love we shower.

Thank you to my friends Violet, Trish, Mitchell, Alice and Maria.
Your presence in my life has opened me up to art and its many wonders.
To my sisters Anna, Amala, and Tara, thank you for being
the rocks which life's storms have allowed me to lean on.
And to my loving parents, Christal and James, thank you the most.
I wouldn't have made it this far without you.

Printed in the United States
by Baker & Taylor Publisher Services